Presented to

Eilidh   fiona   Charnley

by

on

PROMISES
for little hearts

Illustrated by Elena Kucharik

CANDLE
BOOKS

First published in the UK in 1999 by Candle Books
(a publishing imprint of Lion Hudson plc)
Reprinted 2000, 2001, 2002, 2003, 2004
Distributed by Marston Book Services Ltd,
PO Box 269, Abingdon, Oxon OX14 4YN

Worldwide coedition organised and produced by
Lion Hudson plc, Mayfield House,
256 Banbury Road, Oxford OX2 7DH
Tel: + 44 (0) 1865 302750
Fax: + 44 (0) 1865 302757
Email: coed@lionhudson.com
www.lionhudson.com

ISBN 1 85985 266 1

Developed for Tyndale House by The Livingstone Corporation
Prayers by James C. Galvin, Ed.D,

Printed in China.

*C*hildren take promises seriously. If we promise something that we are not able to do, they will most certainly be heartbroken. Consequently, we must be very careful when we make promises to our children.

But we never have to worry about God forgetting his promises. We never have to wonder whether he can fulfill them. The Lord is almighty and dearly loves his children. For these reasons, we can freely teach our children about the promises that God gives to his people. Our children will never be disappointed by him.

The Bible is filled with promises from God. These words reassure us, inspire us, and refresh us. *Promises for Little Hearts* is a collection of some of these cherished passages.

May the Lord bless you and your child as you explore the wonder of the promises in God's Word.

He gives power to those

who are tired and worn out;

he offers strength

to the weak.

Isaiah 40:29

8

Don't be afraid,

for I am with you.

Do not be dismayed,

for I am your God.

I will strengthen you.

I will help you.

Isaiah 41:10

I will lie down in peace

and sleep, for you alone,

O Lord, will keep me safe.

Psalm 4:8

Take delight in the Lord,

and he will give you

your heart's desires.

Psalm 37:4

God is our refuge and strength,

always ready to help

in times of trouble.

Psalm 46:1

When doubts filled my mind,

your comfort gave me

renewed hope and cheer.

Psalm 94:19

Your promise revives me;

it comforts me

in all my troubles.

Psalm 119:50

Your word is a lamp

for my feet and a light

for my path.

Psalm 119:105

When I pray,

you answer me;

you encourage me

by giving me

the strength I need.

Psalm 138:3

When you open your

hand, you satisfy the

hunger and thirst of

every living thing.

Psalm 145:16

The Lord is close to all

who call on him, yes,

to all who call on him

sincerely.

Psalm 145:18

He heals the broken-

hearted, binding up

their wounds.

Psalm 147:3

Commit your work

to the Lord,

and then your plans

will succeed.

Proverbs 16:3

The name of the Lord is a
strong fortress; the godly
run to him and are safe.

Proverbs 18:10

God blesses those who mourn,

for they will be comforted.

Matthew 5:4

Then Jesus said,

"Come to me,

all of you who are weary

and carry heavy burdens,

and I will give you rest."

Matthew 11:28

Jesus said,

"And be sure of this:

I am with you always,

even to the end of the age."

Matthew 28:20

For the proud will be
humbled, but the humble
will be honoured.

Luke 18:14

Jesus said, "I am going to prepare a place for you. . . . When everything is ready, I will come and get you, so that you will always be with me where I am."

John 14:2-3

Jesus said, "Here on earth you will have many trials and sorrows. But take heart, because I have overcome the world."

John 16:33

And we know that God

causes everything to

work together for the good

of those who love God and

are called according to

his purpose for them.

Romans 8:28

So you are all

children of God through

faith in Christ Jesus.

Galatians 3:26

"Honour your father and mother." This is the first of the Ten Commandments that ends with a promise. . . . If you honour your father and mother, "you will live a long life, full of blessing."

Ephesians 6:2-3

51

But the Lord is faithful;

he will make you strong

and guard you from

the evil one.

2 Thessalonians 3:3

For God is not unfair.
He will not forget how hard
you have worked for him
and how you have shown
your love to him.

Hebrews 6:10

55

Be satisfied with what
you have. For God has said,
"I will never fail you.
I will never forsake you."

Hebrews 13:5

If you need wisdom—if you
want to know what God
wants you to do—ask him,
and he will gladly tell you.
He will not resent
your asking.

James 1:5

Give all your worries and

cares to God, for he cares

about what happens to you.

I Peter 5:7

But if we confess

our sins to him,

he is faithful and just

to forgive us and

to cleanse us

from every wrong.

1 John 1:9

See how very much

our heavenly Father loves us,

for he allows us to be

called his children,

and we really are!

I John 3 : I

Thank-You Prayers

Many of us work hard at teaching our children to say thank you when someone does something special for them or gives them a gift. We don't want them to be impolite or ungrateful for the good things they have received. How much more should we teach our children to be grateful to God for the good things he promises to give them every day. Saying thank you to God helps our children count their blessings, and it strengthens their faith. Here are some prayers to help teach your child how to say thank you to God.

MY ROOM

Dear God,

I like my room. Thank you
for giving me such a nice
place to stay. Thank you
also for making a place for
me in heaven. I'm glad
for your promise that
I can stay there someday.
In Jesus' name. Amen.

MY BED

Dear God,

Thank you for my bed.

It helps me feel safe and

warm when I go to sleep.

Help me to make my bed

every morning.

In Jesus' name. Amen.

MY BATH

Dear God,

Thank you for my

bath and my bath toys.

I like smelling the soap

and playing in the water.

Thank you for giving me

a way to stay clean.

In Jesus' name. Amen.

MY TOYS

Dear God,

Thank you for all of my
toys. You gave them to me
so that I can have fun.
Help me to share them with
others. Help me to put them
away after I play with them.
In Jesus' name. Amen.

MY BOOKS

Dear God,

Thank you for all my
books. I love to look at
the pretty pictures and
listen to the exciting stories.
Help me to take good care of
the books I borrow and
the ones I get to keep.
In Jesus' name. Amen.

MY SPECIAL STUFFED TOY

Dear God,

Thank you for my stuffed _____.

I like to have it with me

all the time. Thank you for

your promise to be with me

all the time, too.

In Jesus' name. Amen.

MY CLOTHES

Dear God,

Thank you for my clothes.
They feel comfortable when
I put them on. The special
colours make me look nice.
Thanks for your promise
that I never have to worry
about what to wear.
In Jesus' name. Amen.

MY CRAYONS

Dear God,

Thank you for creating all of the pretty colours in the world. Thank you for giving me crayons and coloured pencils. Thank you for giving me colouring books and blank paper. Help me to be creative, too. In Jesus' name. Amen.

MY DESSERT

Dear God,

Thank you for desserts and snacks. I like these special treats. Help me to eat all of my other food, too.

In Jesus' name. Amen.

MY FRIENDS

Dear God,

Thank you for giving me

friends. I like to play

with them. Help me to be

nice to them. Thank you

for being nice to me.

In Jesus' name. Amen.

77

MY SUNDAY SCHOOL TEACHER

Dear God,

Thank you for my

Sunday school teacher.

Please bless her. Help me

to pay attention so I can

learn more about you.

In Jesus' name. Amen.

MY SAVIOUR

Dear God,

Thank you for sending Jesus

to save us. Thank you that

he wants to be my Saviour.

Please help me to love him

more and more each day.

In Jesus' name. Amen.

ISBN 1 85985 271 8